A Heart Abandoned

Discovering Your Road to Freedom in the Face of a Broken Past

ALLISON HERRIN

RELEVANT
PAGES PRESS

A Heart Abandoned: Discovering Your Road to Freedom in the Face of a Broken Past. Copyright © 2013 Allison Herrin

Unless otherwise indicated, Scripture quotations are taken from the Holy Bible, New International Version®, NIV®. Copyright © 1973, 1978, 1984 by Biblica, Inc.™ Used by permission. All rights reserved worldwide.

Other Scripture references are from the following sources:

The Message. Copyright ©1993, 1994, 1995, 1996, 2000, 2001, 2002. Used by permission of NavPress Publishing Group.

Printed in the United States of America

ISBN-13: 978-0-61587-1-219 (Relevant Pages Press)
ISBN-10: 0-61587-1-216

Cover Design and Photo: Bethany Smith
Author Photo: Carly Jent

MY SINCERE APPRECIATION TO…

My husband Rob, who unselfishly jumped in to my wild and crazy life without ever looking back. I am forever grateful that the LORD saw fit to join you and I as one. You are my HERO!

To my precious, precious boys. You three have endured the hard life with me. It hasn't been easy but I am in AWE of how God is using all of your trials to work ALL things together for good. We will keep running this race together!

A special thanks to my friend and mentor, Julie Hiott, who never gave up on me, even when it might have been easy to do so. You have stood beside me through thick and thin and I am extremely thankful that the LORD gave you to me as a friend. I wouldn't be where I am today without you!

Most important, my sincere and utter gratitude to my Father in Heaven who rescued me from the pit of despair and set me on solid ground in Christ Jesus to ensure that not a shred of my past will have been lived in vain. Your love for me has guaranteed LIFE to the fullest!

Table of contents

Preface

It is undeniable that we simply don't get to where we are without a history. It's really not rocket science. We all have a history, and we have all been shaped by that history, despite our own awareness of it. There are a collection of events in our lives that have contributed to the way we think, feel and behave. As you read and possibly find some correlation to your own life, I am hopeful that you will also find comfort in knowing that you are not alone. Even more so, I hope that I can share some lessons from my own life, and trust that God can use them to help others gain knowledge from my failures and my triumphs to be used for His glory. I am not a psychologist, licensed therapist, social worker, pastor or any of the like. I am simply a child of God whose life has been transformed by His unstoppable power and amazing grace, willing to unlock my past and share my life in hopes that someone else can begin to grasp the power of our Almighty God.

I am a single mom, trying to raise three precious boys into godly young men. Being both mom and dad comes with challenges but God always provides and His love never fails. I was born into a unique family of wounded, broken sinners, not far different from every other family on the planet. After all, we are all sinners living in a broken world, right? Every member of my family has influenced, in some fashion, every other member, and they have all contributed to the shaping of our future. So now it is my turn; to take my story and use it how God wills in the shaping of my little ones and the future that lies ahead for them; wide open and awaiting their arrival.

My prayer is that before you even begin this journey of hope and restoration that God will prepare the soil of your heart for a ripe harvest and although your journey will be much different than mine, I pray that it will be just as extraordinary. I also pray that you will do your part and abandon everything that has been hindering you from coming into the loving, forgiving and capable hands of an enormous and merciful God. He can and will shine into the dark places of our lives and turn our ashes into beauty as we rise up and embrace God, the healer of our heart!

My Prayer for you:

Isaiah 61:1-4

1 The Spirit of the Sovereign LORD is on me,
because the LORD has anointed me
to preach good news to the poor.
He has sent me to bind up the brokenhearted,
to proclaim freedom for the captives
and release from darkness for the prisoners,

2 to proclaim the year of the LORD's favor
and the day of vengeance of our God,
to comfort all who mourn,

3 and provide for those who grieve in Zion—
to bestow on them a crown of beauty

instead of ashes,
the oil of gladness
instead of mourning,
and a garment of praise
instead of a spirit of despair.
They will be called oaks of righteousness,
a planting of the LORD
for the display of his splendor.

4 They will rebuild the ancient ruins
and restore the places long devastated;
they will renew the ruined cities
that have been devastated for generations.

My treasured friend, I pray that this is your year. That God will comfort you and provide for your grief. That He will bestow on you a crown of beauty instead of ashes. That you will no longer mourn or have a spirit of despair but will be covered in gladness and praise. That you will be called righteous because of what the LORD has done and you will display His splendor. I pray that the ancient ruins of your heart will be rebuilt and the devastation that has taken place in your life will be restored and renewed! In Jesus Name!

~ CHAPTER 1 ~

The Wounded Heart

He heals the brokenhearted and binds up their wounds ~Psalm 147:3

I remember it like it was yesterday, yet with vagueness that haunts me. It was a gorgeous October day, but the only thing I recall is being completely and utterly broken, unable to see clearly enough to even notice. I remember sitting on the couch, weeping, trying to figure out what I was going to do next. My life had become such a mess and I had no idea how. I was so broken by the wounds of my past that I couldn't see any logical solution to the chaos that had become my life. I couldn't see my value and my worth. My vision was completely clouded because I had become driven by the negative emotions that had become horribly familiar. I would have done anything to escape them. That was the night I abandoned my short three year marriage. I snuck out the door in the middle of the night with the clothes on my back, two children by my side and one still growing in my womb…only to realize those emotions and wounds traveled right along with me. My marriage was a mess and my husband certainly had his part in the turmoil that now surrounded us, but my emotional and spiritual condition caused me to respond much differently than I would today. What I do know is that our marriage was most definitely going to end in divorce, but not because of that decision on that night.

You see my journey to becoming a single parent didn't begin that night. It didn't begin the day I got married or the day I was divorced. Without question, the journey of my life started long before my existence. Jeremiah 1:5 tells us that before God formed us in our mother's womb He knew us, and before we were born He set us apart. Psalm 139:16 says "…All the days ordained for me were written in your book before one of them came to be." This, my friend, is evidence that the journey of our lives began before we came into the world. My own personal journey has been tainted with many circumstances where the end result was a broken and wounded little girl desperate for security, love and acceptance. Becoming a single parent, for me, was merely an indication of a much bigger crisis within my soul caused by those wounds.

The symptoms of a soul in crisis can range anywhere from fear, anxiety, anger, resentment, depression and more, and these deep wounds can emerge as fear of intimacy, promiscuity, co-dependency, addiction, control and many other behaviors that lead to devastating consequences. However, if we want to begin a journey of restoration, we must go back as far as we can remember and acknowledge our past, because we cannot change it. Instead, we can embrace the truth of our own reality and begin to alter the erroneous beliefs about ourselves and others that we

IF WE WANT TO BEGIN A JOURNEY OF RESTORATION, WE MUST GO BACK AS FAR AS WE CAN REMEMBER AND ACKNOWLEDGE OUR PAST...

have acquired over time through our stained and tarnished lives.

I am certain there is a portion of my family's history that has contributed to my journey that I will never be privy to. There are circumstances that have impacted my family that will not become a part of my memory because they have escaped to the grave with those who partook in them. However, I can wander back to the segments that I do recall; what I can remember and what God has graciously revealed. I can wander back to the fragmented pieces of my past that became important for me to acknowledge. A past that was necessary for me to embrace in order to move forward and hopefully lessen the wounds for my own children as well as the symptoms ignited by those wounds. What little I do know about the generations before me is inadequate to say the least and often I wonder what more there is to discover. I guess it doesn't really matter. If God needs to use it for my benefit or His, I trust that He will reveal it and He will without a doubt do the same for you. What you will unquestionably discover is that this journey of abandoning our hearts completely to the will of God never ends. It is a process of discovery and revelation that brings us to a place of enlightenment where we can begin to identify our symptoms and our behaviors and learn to respond to them from a heart abandoned to God, rather than a wounded hurting heart, because our response is really all that we can control or change.

By the time I was born, my story was already unfolding. Both my mom's and my dad's parents were divorced and consequently, this adventure didn't start well for any of us. I am sure that you have already concluded that my parents ended their marriage as well. Generational sin had a tight hold on my family. Given the circumstances that surrounded them and their respective journeys, my mom and dad did the absolute best possible job that parents could do. After the divorce of my parents, my mom remarried a man who became sexually abusive. I am confident that had she known, she wouldn't have married him. My dad filled his days with drugs, alcohol and women. As children, my siblings and I would visit our father during summer vacation, but most of his time was spent on a boat in the middle of an ocean moving drugs from one place to the next. Yes, my father was a smuggler! By the time I was in middle school my father began a prison sentence that would last until after I graduated high school. I spent every Sunday afternoon of my adolescence visiting him in prison, honestly not knowing at the time how much I really longed for him; yet he was right there in front of me unable to be a father; unable to love his daughter the way she was supposed to be loved by her father. All other days I endured life at home with a great deal of anxiety and fear, wondering if it would ever end. Wondering if this would be the last time my step-father would enter the door to my room. The wall to my heart was closing in and I was powerless to do anything about it. I wasn't even aware that it was happening until much later when the wall became so impenetrable that no one could pierce the entrance to my heart.

You see, when girls grow up without their fathers or with fathers in the home that are physically or emotionally unavailable, the consequences are devastating. I believe that the most important job of our earthly father is to be the image-bearer of God. Before we are able to understand our own faith and rely on God in our own ability, our fathers are supposed to be that for us. They are supposed to show us love the way Christ loves and when we, as women, are not loved and affirmed by our fathers, we will seek it out and find it wherever we can. When that hole in our heart is not filled by our father, we will go to the ends of the earth to find anything that can fill it because we will never feel loved or be satisfied until we do. For me, that search led to sexual and emotional promiscuity that resulted in devastating consequences for my heart. For others, the search leads to addictions that have demoralizing results or maybe isolation which has relational and emotional results. Wherever it leads, at the very core of this search is our desire for deep, lasting love given to us

> *WHEN GIRLS GROW UP WITHOUT THEIR FATHERS, THE CONSEQUENCES ARE DEVASTATING.*

by God himself because He intended it to lead us to Him. He put an imprint on our hearts that can only be filled by His hand. Unfortunately, the search leads us elsewhere because there are wounds delivered by the world in which we live that has led to an emotional and social epidemic evident in the statistics of fatherlessness, addictions, depression, suicide and more, and the consequences are enormous.

There were many trials throughout my childhood that ultimately wounded me so deeply that my heart was literally crumbling. I was dying inside. Oh, on the outside I was the fun girl; the life of the party, but on the inside there was so much pain and turmoil and no one knew it. I am not even sure that I knew. By sharing my life, I hope to provide a clear depiction of a love that conquers ALL through Christ Jesus and offer you a triumph over your own past through His grace. His word will give you practical steps in moving forward into a victorious life where you are no longer victim to your past and your wounds no longer decide who you will become. I share these details because they are the facts that became important for me to acknowledge and the truth of my own reality that I had to come face to face with. I couldn't ignore it and hide behind those walls any longer. I had to decide that I wasn't going to let my past define me as it had done for so many years. While the source of your wounds may be much different than mine, the symptoms are still there. Your wounds may have come as the result of an offense brought on by someone you love. They may be the result of your own errant behavior or the sins of your forefathers that are still affecting your family today. They could be from a disaster, natural or otherwise, or the result of tragedy like losing a loved one to illness, accident or suicide. Or it very well could be just like mine, growing up in a fatherless home and being the victim of abuse. Whatever the cause of your wounds, and we all have them, there is a God that you can retreat to who will support and sustain you. There is a God that can bind up your wounds and heal your broken heart. There is a God that sent His only Son to die for you and suffered until His dying breath so that your heart could ultimately be healed by coming into relationship with your Father God, through Jesus Christ. As we begin this journey together I pray that if you have not already entered into a relationship with Jesus that you will consider it now. It will be the first and most important step on this journey for you to make. I remember the day I gave control of my life to Jesus as if it were yesterday. It wasn't a sight to behold or some miraculous encounter like Paul on the road to Damascus. I simply surrendered myself to Christ one night at a Christian concert because I knew I no longer wanted my life to be what it was and if my life was going to change then maybe this was how. The miracle took place inside where no one else could see. My heart began a journey that night. I had no idea where it would lead, but that decision has been the single most important decision that I have ever

THAT NIGHT, IT WAS AS IF THE WEIGHT OF THE WORLD WAS LIFTED OFF OF MY SHOULDERS. FOR THE FIRST TIME EVER, SOMEONE ELSE HELD ALL OF MY BURDENS...

made and has taken me far beyond where I could have ever imagined. That night, it was as if the weight of the world was lifted off of my shoulders. For the first time ever, someone else held all of my burdens and without carrying that weight I could finally get up and move forward as I began my own journey of healing and restoration. So now it is time to begin yours and who you choose to follow on this journey will be your most important decision ever. Will you let Jesus be your guide? Are you ready to live a life of purpose and hope? God does have a purpose for your life and wants to give you a new beginning. If you find yourself ready to surrender your life to Jesus and allow him to guide you as you begin that relationship with him it's really simple. Just say something like this:

"Father, I know that I am broken and my sins have separated me from you. I am sorry, and now I want to turn away from my past and look toward you. Please forgive me, and help me avoid falling in to sin again. I believe that your son, Jesus Christ, died for my sins, was resurrected from the dead, is alive, and hears my prayer. I invite Jesus to become the Lord of my life, to rule and reign in my heart from this day forward. Please send your Holy Spirit to help me obey You, and to do Your will for the rest of my life. In Jesus' name I pray, Amen!

~ CHAPTER 2 ~

The Feminine Heart

So God created man in His own image, in the image of God He created them; male and female He created them ~ Genesis 1:27

How does one begin the monstrous task of describing such a thing…the feminine heart? It is one of the major intellectual and emotional challenges that we face. *Ask any man.* The heart of a woman is far too intricate for a simple, one sentence definition; too complex and powerful for the ordinary. Women are complex and multifarious and men are simple and uncomplicated. I don't say that in a derogatory manner. It's true. Ask any man and he will tell you how simple they really are and how complicated we can make things.

A HEART ABANDONED

So when I began searching for a description, I enlisted the aid of several friends, men and women, and asked them how they would describe the heart of a woman.

The men very simply said:

"about the size of your fist, pumps blood"

"confusing"

"ummm..."

The women on the other hand had this to say:

"strong, nurturing, selfless"

"caring"

"compassionate"

"courageous"

The dictionary defines the heart in one instance as the center of the total personality, especially with reference to intuition, feeling or emotion. According to the Bible, the heart is the center of spiritual activity and awakening. The heart is the place where the conscience resides (Romans 2:15, Hebrews 10:22). It is naturally wicked and deceitful (Genesis 8:21 and Jeremiah 17:9) and consequently contaminates your character (Matthew 15:18-19, Psalm 73:7) and must be transformed and renewed (Ezekiel 36:26, Psalm 51:10-11.

The question for now however is what makes up the heart of a woman? What drives and motivates her? What desires are inherent in a woman's heart? What are the essentials in the development of a healthy feminine heart? I believe that these answers and many more concerning our hearts are found in the wisdom that comes from God, the one who created it. Not only did He create it, but He fashioned it in His own image! Genesis 1:27 says "so God created man in His own image, in the image of God He created him; male and **female** He created them". I don't know about you, but the thought of that astounds me. God, the creator of the universe and all of its beauty and majesty, made ME, in HIS image. This means that there isn't a thing about me, or you, that He would change or do differently. He wouldn't have me any other way than just the way that I am! Psalm 115:3 says "Our God is in heaven; He does whatever pleases Him". Not only are we made in His image, but we are pleasing to Him. He created us because it pleased Him to do so. During the six days of creation, at the end of every day God would look around at what He created and say to himself "this is good," but did you know that the day He created humans, He responded with "this is VERY good"? He loves us so much. We are the crown of His creation. Even our differences reflect a God who delights in diversity and our hearts are an enormous expression of that uniqueness. God's word says that while man looks at outward appearance, He looks at our hearts.

In His infinite wisdom, God first and foremost created your heart and the heart of every woman to be a dwelling place for Him. Ephesians 3:16-17 says "I pray that out of His glorious riches He may strengthen you with power through His Spirit in your inner being, so that Christ may dwell in your hearts through faith." This describes the God-given hole in every heart that can only be satisfied when He inhabits it. You know this truth. You recognize it. You feel it, even if you can't identify exactly what it is. We search for its fulfillment in many places yet are never satisfied. Without a doubt, our hearts were made to feel and to love others as well, but our love for others is tainted and selfish without our hearts first containing the love of God. Unfortunately, the world today has become so far removed from God that you don't have any idea where to even begin in your search to fill that hole. As you'll ultimately discover, I searched in many places for that fulfillment and never found it until I met Jesus!

> *IN HIS INFINITE WISDOM, GOD FIRST AND FOREMOST CREATED YOUR HEART AND THE HEART OF EVERY WOMAN TO BE A DWELLING PLACE FOR HIM.*

As we learn to turn to God first, allowing Him to fill the gap, He inhabits our heart and it becomes an unveiled place where we are transformed into His likeness. 2 Corinthians 3:15-18 reads:

> *Even to this day when Moses is read, a veil covers their hearts.*
> *But whenever anyone turns to the Lord, the veil is taken away.*
> *Now the Lord is the Spirit and where the Spirit of the Lord is there is freedom.*
> *And we who with unveiled faces all reflect the Lord's glory,*
> *are being transformed into His likeness with ever-increasing glory,*
> *which comes from the Lord, who is the Spirit.*

Do you get that? Whoever turns to the Lord, the veil is taken away. The blinders are removed and truth is revealed. When we turn to the Lord, He gives His Spirit to us and where the Spirit of the Lord is there is freedom. Freedom, my sweet friend! Who doesn't want freedom?

Our God is relational to His core. He loves His creation deeply and desperately wants to be connected with them, to walk with them. In the beginning, before the fall of man, God walked side by side with Adam and Eve in the garden. He physically walked with them! Oh how I have longed for that. If only He were as easily discernible as one who is with me, one that I see, touch, smell, and hear. Maybe this heart thing wouldn't be so difficult to grasp. But the truth is, we live in a fallen world. I have to believe that Adam and Eve didn't know what the temptation and ultimately their sin would do. If they had known the impending consequences of their decision I don't believe their succumbing to the temptation would have been so easy. They wouldn't have believed the lie told them by the enemy that led to the consequences that we still suffer today.

The initial effect of their wrongdoing was shame as they noticed their nakedness for the first time (Genesis 3:7) and ultimately the consequence was separation (Genesis 3:23-24) from God **which is why the heart is so essential**. It is the place where God embeds

> *THE ESSENCE OF A WOMAN CAN ONLY BE UNDERSTOOD IN LIGHT OF COMPARISON WITH GOD HIMSELF.*

our desire for Him. The heart, through Christ Jesus, is the solution to our separation from God. It is the place where He resides, if we let Him. It is where we are transformed and changed into His likeness.

As women, having been created in the image of God, we consequently embody the qualities of God: His beauty and His mystery. We represent His love, His graciousness, His tolerance, His compassion, His kindness and so much more. *The essence of a woman can only be understood in light of comparison with God Himself.*

Deeply ingrained in a woman's heart is her ability to love like no other. We see it in the love that she exhibits for her children. A mother loves unconditionally without hesitation. Her love is unlike any other love on the face of the earth. An unwounded feminine heart has the ability to love without limits. This type of love, this capacity to love, comes from God who placed the ability inside each woman with the intention of exhibiting His fundamental nature. Unfortunately there is not a woman's heart anywhere that remains unwounded. God's word says that ALL have sinned and fall short of His glory and, regrettably, with sin comes hurt and pain. Most of us have encountered circumstances that have wounded us and left us tattered and frail. Some more than others; but no matter the size of your wounds or the significance of the circumstances surrounding your wounds, we all have available to us the ability to let go of our past and move forward into a future full of hope. To gain a heart of restoration and a life of complete fulfillment, however, we must look at that which has been broken. We must encounter our past and identify that which has wounded us so deeply so that we can begin the journey that will thrust us into a life of indescribable joy.

~ Chapter 3~

The Deceived Heart

The thief comes only to steal and kill and destroy ~ John 10:10 ~

I wouldn't go back to my twenties even if it would save my life. I didn't know it at the time but they were the most tumultuous, unhappy times of my life. I spent most of them as a patron of the nightlife as I tried to numb the pain with alcohol and sought attention from any man that was willing to give it. By the time I reached the age of twenty-five, I had slept with well over one hundred men, many of them one night stands. Most of them were perfect strangers. Most nights I was heavily intoxicated because honestly, it was the only way I could go home with someone I had never met. I didn't know it at the time, but my heart was desperately hoping that just one of them would stick around and find me worthy of love, yet because they were strangers they were safe enough not to hurt me too deeply. I was deceived by lies about myself and my worth. I was deceived by lies about men. I was deceived by lies about God. My whole life was a sham.

I share the details of my journey openly hoping that if you see some parallels to your own life, it will begin to open your eyes to your own wounds, since many of us are unacquainted with what we carry deep in our hearts. The walls have hidden our hearts well. These details are what led to my mistaken beliefs that compelled me to make less than perfect decisions that got me to where I am today; a single parent trying to raise three boys completely alone. The events in our lives contribute to the way we think, feel, behave and respond; and they also contribute to the erroneous beliefs that have become a part of who we are. Beliefs that have become so ingrained in us and in our culture that they often go unnoticed.

...MANY OF US ARE UNACQUAINTED WITH WHAT WE CARRY DEEP IN OUR HEARTS.

So how have those events contributed to the way I think, feel, behave and respond? That one question could lead us beyond infinity. There are so many lies that I had come to believe. Many that I still struggle with today. The lies were straight from the wounds of my heart, God's most priceless possession.

The Lies We Believe About Love

The first myth I am certain is the inherent desire of every woman. It is the one thing that we, as women, long for more than anything else. The single thing that when not given to us or shown us properly as a young girl, will escort us into a vile and vicious soul searching that always, always ends in agony and despair unless that searching leads us to the heart of God. This one thing is LOVE! It is the essence of a woman through and through. The desire for love penetrates very deep in the heart of a woman. Depending upon her past, she may give of her heart freely without reservation, and the recipient will be the most blessed man on earth, or she will construct walls around her wounded heart, forbidding love to cross the threshold that she has come to protect so diligently.

So how does it happen? Without any knowledge of their existence, the walls close in and the real woman inside of us, the woman we were meant to be, becomes desperately hidden behind that fortress. How do we get to a point in our lives where we believe the lies about ourselves and about our hearts? Believe the lie that we have to protect ourselves and wall in our hearts so that we don't feel pain again? How do we come to believe the lie that the way to love is through sex and giving away the most sacred part of who we are? We don't do this consciously of course. I wasn't doing it consciously in my early twenties. In fact, most of us are not even aware that we believe such fallacy. Oh, had I only known that it was deceit. If only I had known that I have an enemy who has a vested interest in using every shred of my fragmented past to thrust me into a deep, bottomless pit almost to the point of no return. An enemy that was, and still is, out to devour me *(…your enemy, the devil, prowls around like a roaring lion looking for someone to devour. I Peter 5:8)*.

I have come to understand, in retrospect, that when we, as daughters, are not loved and affirmed by our father, something devastating happens inside of us. A part of us dies and we begin to search for that love and affirmation from wherever we can obtain it. The desire for daughters to be loved by our father is an emotional need deeply rooted in our biological make-up and when gone awry, the consequences are debilitating. My father was not capable of loving me faithfully because of a prison sentence that he endured during the most impressionable time of my life, and my step father loved me during that same time, improperly and immorally. At fifteen, I began to have physical relationships that always ended in heartache. I honestly and naively approached premature sexual relationships with the belief that lasting love would be the outcome. I didn't know at the time that love was what I longed for more than anything else in the world. What happened instead is that every relationship ended, usually pretty quickly, and I began to believe more and more that men were not to be trusted and that I was unworthy of real love and respect. I already clung to that belief through my experiences with my father and my step-father. At nineteen, I began a relationship with a man that I came to love very deeply, or as deeply as was possible for someone as wounded and broken as I was. Nonetheless, he was my first love. When I discovered him in bed with another woman, I was devastated, and once again, the fallacy was confirmed. Men were not to be trusted and I was unworthy. I suppose I had decided somewhere in the realm of my subconscious that I was never going to be vulnerable again. I am not sure when it happened really. Probably long before that particular relationship. That is when I became promiscuous; as friendly as one could be on the outside, but as hard as a rock on the inside. The promiscuity was my way of feeling loved for a moment but guaranteeing that I didn't get close enough to get hurt, yet I was fading fast internally. There was not much left of the real woman. It was all a façade. I had no indication, not a hint of evidence that clued me in to what was happening to me on the inside. In fact, I didn't discover the truth until several years after my divorce, where I found myself broken, wounded and completely ruined emotionally. I was at the very bottom of the pit.

You see, I ended up in this predicament, raising three boys on my own, not because of my ex-husband. Sure he played his part, but I ended up here because I was so desperate for love, the right kind of love, that I said yes to him without any consideration to the strength or health of our relationship. I said yes because we already had a child together out of wedlock and I considered it the right thing to do. I said yes because the walls to my heart were so high, and my heart had become so hardened, that I believed this was all there was for someone like me. After those hundreds of men, he was the first one to stick around longer than a few moments. I said yes, without ever considering what God may have planned for my life. We were both wounded from our past and we could relate to one another. You know the old saying that you attract those who are as healthy as you are? My perception of love was so distorted, I was incapable of making a reasonable and healthy decision. Of course this is all in hindsight. At the time of my divorce, it was HIS mistakes that got us there and I had done nothing wrong. The responsibility of my divorce was not on my shoulder; it was HIS fault and HIS fault alone, yet another symptom of my emotional state of mind. Actually, I ended up in this predicament because of my false belief about love and a wrong response to love within my heart. I got here because I have an enemy who convinced me to believe those fallacies until they became so deeply ingrained that they became a part of who I was. You see, the type of love that God offers and wants for all of us in all of our relationships is far beyond what I had ever learned. It was nothing at all like what I had become acquainted with. So, I believed the fallacy. I still struggle with believing it because Satan will try to use what has worked for him in the past. I understood that love could not be trusted, that love always leaves, always comes to an end. I believed that love was unkind, insensitive and cruel, and I needed to do anything to protect myself from it. The promiscuity was simply my way of hanging on to what little bit of hope was left in my heart, without becoming too vulnerable, because the world told me that sex and love were the same which leads us to the next lie...

The Lies We Believe About Sex

Another lie that I believed and am sure that many young women believe is that sex and love are one in the same. This is about as far from the truth as you can get; yet women still believe that sex will maintain the relationship, will sustain his "love" for her. The only thing that intimacy outside the bounds of a marital relationship will do is bring a throbbing pain that goes deeper than you ever thought possible and has more consequences than you were ever able to imagine. Unfortunately, I know from experience.

I have discovered the hard way that sex is also more than just physical stimulation or a way to show someone you love them, although the world will tell you differently. The world says to do what makes you feel good; it's your body, do with it what you want; it's not hurting anyone and the lies tell us that he will love us more if we give him all of ourselves. What I have discovered is the exact opposite.

> *THE PROBLEM WITH SEX OUTSIDE OF MARRIAGE IS THAT IT IS A SCAM. IT RESEMBLES TRUE INTIMACY BUT IT IS NOTHING OF THE LIKE.*

You see, the problem with sex outside of marriage is that it is a scam. It resembles true intimacy but it is nothing of the like. It makes you believe that the intimacy within the relationship is more than what it really is. Premarital sex uses the language of love and commitment, but knows nothing of either one. At our deepest level, we crave that true intimacy. That is, after all, what that hole in our heart that we desperately seek to fill is. It is the God-given hole in our heart that He designed in each of us that would hopefully lead us to Him. But instead of choosing Him, we spend countless hours, days, or even years choosing others, choosing sex, seeking love in the world, or hiding from it because of the pain, rather than allowing Him to love us in the only way that will fill that space in our hearts.

You see, I spent many, many years looking for love in all the wrong places. I was drinking seven nights a week because it was the only way to numb the pain. I spent at least five of those nights in someone else's bed, usually a stranger, because it was the only way to relieve the loneliness. The pain of my past had caused so much emotional turmoil that I began feeling lonely, rejected, angry, and resentful. I would have said yes to anyone so I could feel the euphoria of love just for a moment. What I didn't know is that ecstasy wouldn't last and in fact it wasn't real at all. I was being lied to by the enemy of my soul. I didn't know that God was the only one who could cure all the turmoil inside. I didn't even know that ultimately, God is who I was actually searching for. Not love. God is love and if we find Him we unmistakably find love.

The Lies We Believe About Happiness

In addition to looking for love in the wrong places, many of us, including myself, have spent a lifetime searching for happiness. We pursue it in things like affluence, titles, family, fame, sex, love, friends, and so much more, yet somehow we still never seem to be satisfied. We always want more because we are just not as happy as we thought we would be once we have attained those things. I know that we as women tend to search for happiness in things like love and the ability of another to fulfill us. Or we seek happiness by pursuing external beauty at any cost. Unfortunately our idea about love is elusive to say the least. Our blurred perception of happiness and love has been formed not only through the media but also through our experiences with others and how we have been treated and cared for by those who "love" us. We have come to believe that love is a physical and emotional response in our attraction to another. This is certainly a minute part of it that should be contained within marital bounds but it encompasses so much more, at least from God's point of view. Our belief about beauty has been shaped by Hollywood and the media who have told us nothing but lies. We have been told, directly and indirectly, that beauty is on the outside; what we look like. We have come to believe that if we are beautiful enough or have the kind of figure she has or weighed the same as she does, then, and only then, will we be happy. Or perhaps if we find Prince Charming and he rescues us from our mediocre existence then, just maybe, we will be happy. You see, women want more than anything in the world to be affirmed and to be loved. It is a God-given desire designed to lead us to Him. Unfortunately, through movies, television, magazines and the like, we have come to believe that affirmation comes from physical beauty, and let's face it, men have not been prone to treat us much differently because of their own personal battles. In the same respect many of us have come to believe that love is something that we feel, an emotion that is fleeting and can be here today and gone tomorrow. We believe that if we are no longer happy in our marriage then we must not be in love any longer, or if we are no longer fulfilled then the love has disappeared. Unfortunately, this belief has led to the highest divorce rate in history.

Regardless of how we have sought happiness, if we have searched in the wrong places, I believe that we will eventually, if we haven't already, end in same place; still completely and utterly dissatisfied. Why is that? Why is it that we can gain everything that we have aspired to and worked so hard for yet still be thoroughly unhappy and discontent? Why is it that once we get to where we want to be we discover that it is not enough? Why do we

THE PROBLEM IS THAT WE GET TO THE OTHER SIDE OF THE FENCE ONLY TO FIND THAT IN ORDER TO HAVE GREENER GRASS YOU MUST BE WILLING TO CARE FOR IT.

always want more? I believe it is because we are mistaken in our beliefs about what actually fulfills us. We believe in chasing that which is tangible, well, because it's tangible. Besides, it's what everyone else does. We honestly have become a generation that doesn't know any better. We chase the tangible because we are self-centered. Why? Maybe because our parents made us the center of their world, allowing us actions with no consequences, believing that it was best. To no fault of their own, they were just heeding the advice of the "experts" of their time. Or maybe it's because of the age we live in, where we have anything and everything available to us with the click of a button. Or, we chase tangible things because consumerism has gone so wrong in our society, noted by the idea that he who has the most money wins, so we pursue riches to make us happy. We chase tangible love because Hollywood has perverted sex and love so much so that we now believe that it doesn't matter who it's with as long as you are happy and your needs are being met. Are you not happy with your current husband? Just get yourself another one. Are you not happy with men? Go find a woman. The idea of the grass being greener on the other side has become so ingrained in us that we are in hot pursuit of the other side of the fence, believing that this is where we will find happiness. I would guess that this could possibly be the explanation for over 50% of marriages ending in divorce, leaving the same percentage of children growing up in single parent homes. The problem is that we get to the other side of the fence only to find that in order to have greener grass you must be willing to care for it. It must be watered, aerated, fertilized, mowed and genuinely cared for if it is going to be as green as you had hoped. If only we had known before we jumped the fence, maybe we would have cared for what was already in our own yard. Maybe we would have put more time into our own marriages and family rather than pursuing a better one or pursuing things that could possibly make us happier.

So where do we find true happiness? I can say with 100% certainty that you will not ever find it in another person. Yet that's what we do. We look for someone else to make us happy and when they no longer do, we leave —self-centeredness at its best. Now let me say with utmost sincerity that this is not to condemn anyone for their current situation or where they have been. I promise you, I have been there too. This is to shed some light on the truth and inhibit us from making the same mistakes again and again, and hopefully prevent our own children from procuring the same fate.

Your response to your own past and the lies that you have come to believe may not look the same as mine. Your response may have been isolation where you have spent your life alone or at least far from intimate relationships. Maybe you have had the habit of choosing destructive relationships where your partner was physically or emotionally abusive. Or maybe you've decided that women could be trusted more than men so you have turned to lesbian relationships, even though you know deep inside that this is not God's plan for you. For most of us, we don't even know that we have made these choices out of heartache. I know that I believed I was just having fun. I believed that I really wanted to have sex with more men than I care to count because I was just having fun and being independent just like the world told me I should be. I had no idea I was actually trying to fill a void; no idea that my past had wounded me so deeply. One thing I can stand here and tell you, however, is that no matter how you have chosen to fill the void or soften the wounds and no matter how those choices have hardened your heart, and believe me, they have — There is hope, my friend!

~ Chapter 4 ~

The Awakened Heart

But whenever anyone turns to the LORD,
the veil is taken away
~ 2 Corinthians 3:16 ~

Now that some lies have been exposed and we have discovered the tactics of the enemy, let's remove the veil and discover some truths that can only be found in the Word of God.

The Truth About Love

LOVE; the word is so limited. The truth of love is so vast, so immeasurable, that we could spend an eternity searching for its meaning and still never comprehend genuine, authentic love the way God intended it. What I have discovered is the kind of love we search for and deeply long for can only be found in one place. My heart, and yours, can only be protected by one person. When we build those walls around our heart, our heart becomes a place that welcomes no one, not even the one Prince that can rescue us and truly love us, Jesus. I John 3:16 says "This is how we know what love is: Jesus Christ laid down His life for us..." That's it! Don't you see that's where true love begins? Friends, until we embrace how wide and how deep the love of God is for us, we will not ever come close to loving others the way He intended. Once we truly come to understand that God's love is unconditional, enduring, sacrificial, unending, unfailing, forgiving and all-powerful, then and only then are we able to take the next step appropriately and naturally: the step of obedience. Obedience is where God's love is perfected in us. I John 2:5 says "But if anyone obeys His word, God's love is truly made complete in Him". So you see, love is not the emotions we feel. They are too fleeting, always coming and going. True love comes from our dedication to God that stems from understanding His deep love for us.

Love is always a choice, an act of our will. In Hosea Chapter 3 you read the story of Hosea and Gomer. Gomer was a prostitute who kept leaving her husband to return to prostitution. God told Hosea in verse 1 "Go show your love to your wife again, though she is loved by another and is an adulteress. Love her as the LORD loves the Israelites, though they turn to other gods…" and he did it! I believe Hosea obeyed out of his dedication to God, not out of an emotional love for his wife. How many of you could keep returning to an adulterer? I will never forget, one summer I was dating a man whom I cared very deeply for. As I was praying about our relationship, the LORD told me very clearly that I was going to love this man without expecting anything in return. WHAT??? How can I love someone who might not love me back? Yet that is what Jesus does for us every single day. Once I really knew that this was what God was calling me to do, this was the prayer I wrote in my journal:

> *UNTIL WE EMBRACE HOW WIDE AND HOW DEEP THE LOVE OF GOD IS FOR US, WE WILL NOT EVER COME CLOSE TO LOVING OTHERS THE WAY HE INTENDED.*

You have asked me to love him without expectations, to love him no matter the pain. I do this only because you ask; because I know your plans are good. I need your wisdom LORD. I am not sure I know how to do this. In each situation I need your strength to ask "what does love look like here?" Guide me LORD. More than anything, I want to honor you and obey you. You have been so faithful in showing me your ways. Give me strength to be faithful in what you are asking of me. Forgive me when I fail.

I didn't know for sure what this was going to look like. All I knew was that I wanted to honor and obey a God that had been faithful to me. He used that summer to teach me many things, but most of all, through my obedience, He gave me a broader understanding of what love is. Here is what I came to discover through that relationship as I allowed God to teach me: Love is not about feelings, although they are certainly a part of it. God created us with those emotions. True love, however, is about a choice to love someone no matter what. No matter what they do, how they look, what they say or how they hurt you. This is why the person that you CHOOSE to love for life should not be taken lightly. When you say for better or for worse in your marriage vows, don't let them be just empty words. When God told me that I was going to love this man without expectation, I arrogantly thought that He was going to use me to show His love to someone else. I was thrilled and honored. What I didn't know is that it had nothing to do with the guy at all. It had to do with what the LORD wanted to teach me. God wanted me to choose to love this man no matter what my emotions told me. No matter how he may have hurt me and through that God showed me this inexplicable truth: IT IS JUST AS WRONG FOR ME TO BE IN A RELATIONSHIP WITH SOMEONE BECAUSE OF HOW I FEEL ABOUT THEM AS IT IS TO LEAVE A MARRIAGE BECAUSE OF HOW I FEEL AT THE MOMENT. Do you get that? I mean, I know it's wrong to leave a marriage because of feelings that are fleeting, but it's wrong to even start one with feelings? I don't know about you, but every relationship I have ever been in was because of a feeling that I was responding to. If I didn't feel it, I wasn't in it, but that is not how God wants us to love. In the same respect, just because we feel it doesn't mean that God wants us in it either. I have clung to so many relationships because my feelings were too strong to let go. Even if I was treated poorly, I would continue to stick around because the pain of being hurt was much less than the pain of letting go. Oh, how little I valued myself. I don't know about you, but lessons for me are always painful. I am a little hard-headed and strong-willed to say the least. I always seem to learn lessons the hard way. This lesson of love I, without a doubt, have learned the hard way. Unfortunately I am not finished yet either. Though that relationship ended very painfully, God used it to help me understand another layer in this very deep thing called love. I hope and pray that I don't have to go through another painful relationship in order to learn more but I am confident that if I do, it will be well worth it in the end. Here is what I don't want you to miss friends. Just because it is difficult or painful does not mean that God is not in it. The key here is to have our hearts where they belong, even in the midst of pain and difficulty; completely abandoned to the will of God. He is so tender in the midst of pain and completely faithful to teach us His ways, but we must let Him. He will not push it on us but if we open up to Him, He will not fail!

So what does love look like? For me, that summer, it simply looked like obedience. I had finally come to the realization that my own love was not enough, so all I knew was I wanted to do it differently. I had prayed a couple of years prior, in the midst of another failed relationship, that God would show me what true love was because I kept messing it up and guess what? He was showing me. He is still showing me. He is so faithful to answer our prayers, but He will not force our response. Just as we teach our own children and long for them to make the right choices, so God teaches us His ways as He longs for us to choose to follow. Obedience is not easy if we don't understand love, but once we grasp the greatness of God's love and turn our hearts to Him, obedience and dedication follow. Our will becomes choosing to love Him and to love others the way He does.

You see, when true love manifests, it is patient and kind, not unwilling and cruel as I had learned. True love is not proud and does not boast, but humble and modest. I was anything but. It is not rude or self-seeking, yet everyone I had come in close contact with in my past was one or the other, if not both. True love is not easily angered. I was justifiably about as angry as any one person could be, but the anger was devouring my soul. True love does not delight in evil, as my step father had shown me; it rejoices in the truth, as I have now become acquainted with through the vast, abounding love of Jesus Christ.

The Truth About Sex

It took me a long time to understand that God's instructions for sex are not prohibitive but guidelines designed to protect us; protect our mind, body, soul and our dignity, as well as protect the one we are with. They are guidelines that will thrust us into our God-given roles as women that will honor Him as well as honor the one that will eventually become our spouse.

What I have finally come to understand is that sex is the most intimate and ultimate of all human giving and vulnerability. Sex does feel good, but hurts more deeply than you can ever imagine when you partake in it outside of a committed marital union. Yes, it is your body, but not to do with what you want. It is a body given as a gift from our Creator meant to be a holy vessel through which He can serve His purposes that are always intended for your good. Through this one act of intimacy, we give ourselves so fully to one another that it only seems right that it take place in a union of total surrender between two people who have given themselves completely—body, mind, and spirit—to one another. I have come to understand, through personal experience as well as a Christian conviction, that to give someone your body, without giving the rest of you, your mind (a conscious choice of commitment) and your spirit (your emotions and affections), is to separate the physical from the rest of the components of your being, which literally rips us to pieces at the depths of our soul. When God says that the two become one, He really means it. Premarital sex divides us at our deepest level, giving out a part of us, without giving out the rest intended to go with it, and we wonder why intimate relationships hurt so badly when they come to an end. It is because we truly do become one flesh and when the relationship comes to an end we are ripped apart, left with an open, gaping wound. I am not sure where any of us, much less myself, have gotten the idea that we can do whatever we want with one part of our being, our bodies, and believe that there are no consequences for the other parts of our being. I unfortunately have lived those consequences because I was not taught that sexual intimacy was a beautiful and remarkable act created by God himself for true intimacy with your spouse. In fact, I was taught and treated like quite the opposite, as you have come to discover.

> GOD'S INSTRUCTIONS FOR SEX ARE NOT PROHIBITIVE, BUT GUIDELINES DESIGNED TO PROTECT US

I have had to come to my own convictions and the reality of premarital sex the hard way. My prayer is that you don't have to do the same. I am speaking to single women here. We cannot keep going through relationships believing that sexual intimacy will keep it together. It takes so much more. We can't keep believing when he says he will be there tomorrow that he will be, and our way to ensure that is to show him how much we love him by giving all of ourselves to him. It doesn't work. I promise. Believe me: I have made all the excuses in the world of why *this guy* is different. But the reality

is that it is not about the guy at all. It is about who you are in Christ
and the plan that He has for your life and your purity. I beg of you to
keep the most sacred part of yourself in the hands of God. It is the
only safe place for it to remain until your man of God comes and
takes you into his arms in a permanent union the way God designed
it. Anything other than that only brings heartache and despair. And
for married women, this incredible act of intimacy is not something
to be used as a pawn for you to get what you want or need in your
relationship. It is too precious a gift to be used as a tool of
manipulation. God is bigger than our feelings and He can help us
begin to understand the depth and width of His love for us for the
purpose of loving others, including our husbands and the way He
would have us love them. Sex is an act of intimacy created by God
Himself for the purpose of multiplying, yes, but at its deepest level it
puts us in a place of vulnerability, intimacy and trust that cannot be
understood or perfected anywhere else than under the umbrella of
God's will, in marriage.

The Truth About Happiness

Happiness is defined in the dictionary as being characterized
by or indicative of pleasure, contentment or **joy**. In order to be
characterized by something, whatever it is, it has to become a part of
who you are as a person. It will begin to define you and whatever it is
that's going on around you cannot change this characterization. Does
this mean that if you are characterized by joy that you will never be
sad? Absolutely not! It simply means that the sadness does not define

who you are. It does not become a part of you or drive what you do, say, think or believe. Where joy lives, sadness cannot hang around for long. We will without a doubt feel sadness in this world, but it cannot survive if we are characterized by joy.

So where does this joy come from? How do we seek it? How do we become characterized by it? We do so by abandoning our hearts to the will of God and believing that He has our best interest in mind. By believing that He knows better than we do the path that is right for us and the path will bring us the full joy that is available to us. But we can't just believe it. We must behave like we believe it. In every circumstance we must pray and ask God what He thinks is best and be willing to obey when He answers. We must read His word and obey His commands, not necessarily

SEEK GOD FIRST AND YOU WILL INEVITABLY FIND JOY; EVEN IF JOY IS NOT WHAT YOU ARE SEARCHING FOR

with the idea that He is being prohibitive, but with the belief that it is for our protection coming from a Father who loves us deeply. It really is that simple. Seek God first and you will inevitably find joy; even if joy is not what you are searching for. Nehemiah 8:10 says that the very source of our strength comes from the joy that is only available from the LORD. This joy does not come from our situation or circumstances. It doesn't come from our emotional state and how we feel at the moment. Satan has deceived us into believing that when this particular trial is over or when we obtain a bigger home or get a promotion or our husband or child changes or maybe when we lose 18 pounds, then our joy will be complete. But God says our joy is in Him and is available to us right now, right at this very moment. Not tomorrow, not when you are healed, not when your sorrow has passed but right now.

I challenge you to take some time to seek Him and draw near to Him in worship and prayer. Dive in to His Word and discover His plan for your life. Discover His commands that will guide you and protect you. Here is where you will become characterized by joy. Here is where you will find unrelenting strength. Here is where you will find the true meaning of happiness.

John 15:10-12
If you obey my commands, you will remain in my love, just as I have obeyed my Father's commands and remain in His love. I have told you this so that my joy may be in you and that your joy may be complete.

So you see, it doesn't end there, in the pit of despair. For me, it ends in a saving knowledge of the One who loves me unconditionally. It ends with the One who set me free from the lies. It ends with the One who has healed my heart and knows me more intimately than anyone ever will. It ends with Jesus. But it doesn't really end there. It has only begun…

~Chapter 5~

The Circumcised Heart

Circumcise your hearts, therefore, and do not be stiff-necked any longer
~ Deuteronomy 10:16 ~

Circumcision is not necessarily an exciting procedure to consider. If you are a mom of boys, you know how excruciating it can be. Painful yes, but said to protect from certain diseases and complications. In the same way, circumcising the heart or cutting away that which causes complications is a necessary part of this journey of abandoning our hearts.

The Message Bible says it like this: "So cut away the thick callouses from your heart and stop being so willfully hardheaded."

As we've undoubtedly discovered, wounds in this life cause pain and with pain comes scars and with scars, callouses. God tells us to cut them away, like a foreskin. In fact, the King James Version literally says to cut away the foreskin of your heart.

Our hearts are full of emotional wounds that have clouded our minds as well as cluttered the space in our hearts. Our hearts have become hardened or calloused because of the pain of our past and because we have become so hardened we have become less and less sensitive to others and more importantly, less and less sensitive to God. This callousness has made us stubborn, rebellious and foolish, and has caused us to resist the Holy Spirit, and many of us don't even know it. All we know is the pain.

To understand circumcision of the heart, we must first understand the significance of circumcision of the flesh. Throughout the Old Testament circumcision represented many things to God's chosen people. It represented a covenant or a promise between the people of God and God Himself, it represented their identity as God's people and in Joshua chapter 5 it clearly states that you could not enter the Promised Land unless you were circumcised. God's Word is timeless and full of great treasures that we can learn from. I would argue that in the same way, the circumcision of our hearts represents the very same. At some point, we all face God as uncircumcised, un-renewed sinners in search of truth. It is by faith in Christ that His Spirit will circumcise your heart and His Spirit will give birth to new life within you.

When our hearts are circumcised and we surrender it all and open our hearts to Jesus, the New Covenant is established: a promise from God himself that He will forgive your sins and all of your past as you come into relationship with Him. And as you take that step with God, through Christ Jesus, the callouses, the fortress that you have built, that have been your defense mechanism to the pain, are cut away and the healing hand of Christ can now reach those once walled-in places and begin the therapeutic process of restoration. This is His covenant, His promise. Isaiah 61 says that He will rebuild the ancient ruins and restore the places long devastated. Has your heart been devastated sweet friend? Jesus can restore it! Psalm 30:2 says that you can call for God's help and He will heal you! Psalm 103:3 says that He forgives ALL your sins and heals ALL your diseases. The Psalms also say that He heals the brokenhearted and binds up their wounds. Circumcision is painful, but there is healing that follows. Allow Jesus to invade those places in your heart that need healing and cut away those callouses; break down those walls. How? Just open your heart to Him (see pg. 20).

Circumcision also represented the Jew's identity as God's chosen people. It was the outward sign of an inward promise. In Acts chapter 15 Peter is speaking to the Pharisees who demanded that Gentiles (non-Jews) are circumcised as well. He says:

> *"Brothers, you know that some time ago God made a choice among you that the Gentiles might hear from my lips the message of the gospel and believe. ⁸ God, who knows the heart, showed that He accepted them by*

giving the Holy Spirit to them, just as He did to us. 9 He made no
distinction between us and them, for He purified their hearts by faith".

You see, your identity, sweet sister, is in Jesus, not in what you are on
the outside. God knows your heart and He accepts you just the way
you are and He shows that by giving you the Holy Spirit to be your
guide. He makes no distinction between you and anyone else and He
will purify your heart. He will cut away all that hinders your growth
and your ability to live your life to the fullest. But you have to
choose Him. You have to say yes and open that window to your
heart that has been walled-in for so long so He can begin His
miraculous work within.

If you are in a relationship, your heart must be involved
right? Your heart must belong to the relationship or the relationship
itself will eventually die. Circumcision is the tool that God uses to
cut away everything in your heart that is keeping you from loving
God. This process has been one of the most painful things that I
have endured in my walk with the LORD, however on the other side,
my devotion and love for God are stronger than ever and our
relationship has become magnificent. I know Him deeper than I ever
thought possible and you can too.

The last thing that circumcision represented in the Old
Testament was the Promised Land. In Joshua chapter 5 God clearly
would not allow them to enter into the Promised Land until they
were circumcised. In same way, I believe that our hardened and
calloused hearts, our uncircumcised hearts, prevent us from living in

our promised land. The hardness causes doubts as we allow Satan to convince us of lies about God and others that simply aren't true, and in turn we keep people and God at arms distance. By doing so, we aren't living life to fullest as God promised in John 10:10. He says that "the thief comes only to steal and kill and destroy; I have come that they may have life, and have it to the full".

Are you keeping yourself at arms distance from the world to ensure you don't get hurt again? Are you being rebellious, knowing that you are living in sin but choose to stay there anyway? Are you living in doubt, not believing that you were created by God, in His image, for a purpose? Is your heart calloused as a defense mechanism to the pain that you feel?

The Word says that we are to serve the LORD God with all of our heart but how do we give Him all of our heart if it is calloused over and full of junk?

I remember a time that I was struggling to trust God for my provision. After all, I had been homeless, evicted on several occasions and often had to forgo buying something like shampoo or paper towels so that I could afford food for my family. My heart was hardened in the area of provision. One day, my oldest son, Cameron was in 5th grade. He had a science project due the next day. I remember pulling up to the gas station only to discover that I didn't even have the ninety-five cents that it was going to cost for a twenty ounce Coca-Cola. He needed the bottle for the project. I began ripping my car apart, hopeful that I would find some change under the seats. I didn't. I began weeping and crying out to God: "Why are things so hard, God? Why can't you just provide for me? I don't ask for much." After sitting in the car for what seemed like hours, crying and wondering what I was going to do, I walked into the gas station with every intention of asking for a Coke on credit. I would promise to come back and pay for it next week when I got paid. The clerk saw my despair, evident from the mascara all over my face, and came over to console me. I told her the story and she offered to buy the Coke for me. I said no several times (pride was another area that had hardened my heart) but she insisted. I remember walking back out to the car in disbelief. Had my life really come to this? Was this how it was going to be for me and my children? I sat in the car and began crying some more: "God, if he (my ex-husband) would just pay child support, we would be ok and we wouldn't struggle like this". God very clearly said to me that day *"He is not your provider, I am!"* ~ "Then why aren't you providing for me?' ~ *"I just did, didn't I?"*

You see, God used that day to remove some of the callousness, to cut away some of the hardness that was keeping me from trusting in Him. I wanted Him to provide my way. He wanted to teach me His ways and because I was open to receive His discipline that day, I had the painful honor of having one more callous stripped away.

I remember the summer of 2008. My children and I had been working diligently on the home that we were building. Going to the construction site day after day, chipping away at what was to be our very own home. We were so excited to finally have the opportunity to have stable housing and break the cycle of eviction that had become so familiar. The problem was, I wouldn't let anyone help. I didn't want anyone to know. I was buying my home from Habitat for Humanity and because of pride I was mortified at the thought of letting anyone know that I wasn't buying this home by myself. Pride was another area that had a tight hold on my heart. I had been hurt so much in my life; I think I needed to prove to the world that I didn't need anyone. That way I wouldn't get hurt. Again, I was letting no one in. As God would have it, in order to seal the deal with Habitat for Humanity, I had to be willing to tell my story. That summer, my face was plastered all over the news, the local paper, magazines and speaking engagements. God was going to break down that wall of pride that had produced a calloused heart. And again, I had the painful honor of yet another callous being stripped away from my hardened heart.

You see, as painful as it has been, and there have been many other circumstances that have stripped away at my heart, I have found freedom on the other side of the pain. Needless to say, this is a long, painful process well worth the pain as our hearts learn to obey out of our deep love for our Father God because of the love He showers on us.

I challenge you to open your heart to Jesus and then allow the Holy Spirit to strip away the callouses that have hardened your heart. Take responsibility for allowing the enemy to deceive you. Practice regular confession to keep the callouses from rebuilding and placing you in bondage again. Read the Word of God regularly. Hebrews 4:12 says that *the Word of God is alive and active. Sharper than any double-edge sword, it penetrates even to dividing soul and spirit, joints and marrow; It judges the thoughts and attitudes of the heart.* So you see, God uses the Sword of The Spirit, The Word of God, to circumcise our hearts but He can't use it if you are not reading it and studying it. David says in the Psalms, "I hide your word in my heart that I might not sin against you". He hid God's word in his heart by reading and meditating on it. Also, pray, pray and pray again as you begin to allow the LORD to remove those callouses, understanding that it might be painful. Ask God to remove the unwanted nature of your flesh and circumcise your heart so that you may enter into a more intimate relationship with Him. You may just have to go back as far as you can remember and face your past in order to face the pain head on and deal with it. Just as in physical circumcision, there is a healing time, but know this; **you are not dealing with your past alone**. Our God is greater than any of that pain and He desperately desires for you to move beyond it to a life of freedom as He gently guides you to the places you need to go. As He gently circumcises your heart and opens it up again to begin the healing process.

~ Chapter 6~

The Healed Heart

He heals the brokenhearted and binds up their wounds ~ Psalm 147:3 ~

Now that we have uncovered some truth about our past, exposed the callouses and revealed some of the fallacies that we have come to believe, what do we do about it? How do we change the way we think, feel, behave and respond? How do we break down the walls surrounding our hearts? How do we change the habits that are deeply attached to those lies? Again, I am certain the answers are found in the truth of God's timeless Word.

As we have journeyed together, most of us have undoubtedly come to recognize that we all have wounds. It's impossible to go through life without them. They come from living in a sinful world and with sin, comes pain. Yes, some sins are more heinous than others, but all sins cause wounds nonetheless. We cannot allow our hurts, no matter the magnitude, to be minimized to unworthy of our attention and God's healing touch. So how do we begin to heal those wounds? How do we make the shift from old beliefs into new beliefs, from darkness into light? For me, it began with my willingness to open my heart to God; to **receive His love**. I had to take the first step. Sure, God is big enough and quite capable of forcing me to love Him and open up to Him, but that would make Him no different than my step-father. It would make Him no different than an abusive husband or a rapist for that matter, and that is not the God I know. The God that I have become intimately acquainted with is a gentleman who loves deeper than we can imagine. A Father who would do anything and sacrificed everything to show you how wide and deep His love is for YOU. Amy Carmichael, a missionary to India in the early 1900's, wrote:

> *There is no need to plead that the love of God shall fill our hearts as though He were unwilling to fill us. He is willing, just as light is willing to flood a room that is open to its brightness.*

Think about it... When you open the blinds in a room, light automatically comes in but when the blinds remained closed the light remains at the window but doesn't enter the room. It's still there, just not in that room. In the same way, God remains at the window of our heart, waiting for us to open so that He can flood the room of our heart with His great love. You see, God will not force His love on us, but He is always waiting for us to open our hearts and invite Him in.

This love thing, especially the love of God, is so hard to grasp. We have diluted the word love so much that we can't even begin to comprehend it. Or we've been hurt so deeply that we don't know how to receive it.

Maybe you are someone who feels as if God has abandoned you. How could He let the things that have happened to you take place? Where was He when you were suffering so deeply? Where was He when your dad walked out? When your husband left? Where was He when you lost your child? When your best friend moved away? Where was He when you were being abused? When you got sick? Insert whatever situation you have found yourself in. I have wrestled with these very same questions and more. My answer to you is HE HAS ALWAYS BEEN THERE. Feelings aside, He has always been there!! Unfortunately in this life there will be events and circumstances imposed on us beyond our will. There is evil in this fallen world. **Even Jesus was betrayed by those that He trusted most**. Those who have imposed their will on us and have hurt us will be held accountable for their actions. Maybe not in this world, but they, and everyone else, will answer to God one day. What we are responsible for is how we respond.

No matter how we have responded up to this point, our next step and undoubtedly the hardest step of all is **forgiveness**. I know it seems impossible but I promise it's not. It is a leap of faith and an act of your will. Ask God for help. I remember the day I forgave my step-father like it was yesterday. I was nineteen years old and had taken my first step of opening my heart to Jesus just a few months prior. I knew he was coming to visit and had been asking God to help me respond the way He would have me respond. I opened the door to my home and before I could do anything else, I hugged his neck and said "I forgive you." It was not planned, it just happened. It wasn't until ten years later that I realized that this was my first supernatural experience. There is no way on the face of the planet that I was even ready to consider forgiving him, much less actually do it, yet because I prayed a simple prayer for God to help, He intervened. In hindsight, I now know that God allowed that experience to show me what forgiveness looks like. He used it to show me what it felt like. The heaviness was lifted almost immediately. He used it to clearly show me that forgiveness was for me and not for the person responsible for hurting me. He knew that there would be many more opportunities along the way for me to choose to forgive. I will tell you without a doubt that you cannot begin your journey of restoration until you choose to forgive. Unforgiveness is so powerful that it can literally stop you in your tracks on the road to healing and restoration. Here is something that I want to make very clear: Forgiveness does not set the perpetrator, free it sets YOU free. Anger and bitterness disappear in the face of forgiveness. God says that "as far as the east is from the west, I will forgive you" and He calls us to do the same.

I John 2:6 says that if we claim to live in Him and love Him then we must walk as Jesus walked. Did you know that as Jesus was being crucified, nailed to a cross, His words were "Father forgive them for they know not what they do"? I am not saying that this is easy. In fact it is quite the opposite. Learning to forgive is one of the hardest things you will ever face but God is faithful and will use that forgiveness to set you free from your past. Ask Him to show you how to forgive. It will change your life. I promise!

The third step in healing your wounds is allowing God to take your now open and clean heart and saturate it with **His love**. Unfortunately, for many years, I believed that my healing in the area with my step-father was complete. I believed that forgiving my step-father had healed me. I mistakenly believed that forgiveness and healing were one in the same. My friend, I cannot stress enough that they are not!

FORGIVENESS DOES NOT SET THE PERPETRATOR FREE, IT SETS YOU FREE

You can forgive without healing but you cannot heal without forgiving. I came to this realization several years ago when my step-father's name appeared on Facebook wanting me to confirm him as a friend. I hadn't seen or heard from him in over 20 years. The minute I saw it, without thought, I became hysterical. I dropped to my knees in a public park and sobbed for a half an hour in pain simply at the sight of his name. I spent the next few days crying out to God: "Why did I respond that way? Why does this still hurt so bad 20 years later?" It was then that I realized my healing was not

A HEART ABANDONED

complete. I was still so wounded that I couldn't even conjure up the courage to open Facebook until several weeks later. When I finally did, the request was still there waiting for me to confirm.

YOU CAN FORGIVE WITHOUT HEALING BUT YOU CANNOT HEAL WITHOUT FORGIVING

When I opened it up, I had no idea who the man in the picture was. Praise God, it was not my step-father. What I do know, however, is that God used that unpleasant event to show me that there was more healing to take place in this wounded heart and as painful as that was, I am so glad that He has used something as small as a friend request on Facebook to bring my healing onto the path of completion. You see, He can use anything, big or small, as a tool to bring healing to your heart too.

So how do we begin to allow God to saturate us with His indescribable love? Psalm 136 speaks incessantly about the fact that God's love endures forever. No matter what we have done or what others have done to us, HIS love endures FOREVER! The love of God is so wide and so deep and until we allow Him to soak us with it, we will not find healing for our wounds. It's like allowing a broken arm to heal without a cast. The bone heals crooked and causes more problems than it did before. Psalm 147:3 says "He heals the brokenhearted and binds up their wounds." The word bind in the dictionary has several meanings:

- To tie or encircle
- To bandage
- To unite
- To finish
- To restrain
- To shackle

Oh sweet friend, do you see it? Close your eyes and imagine the wounds that are within your heart. Now imagine God putting a bandage around them or restraining them from hurting you and holding you back any longer. Imagine Him shackling your wounds and not ever letting them loose on you again! Do you know that the opposite of bind is to set free or loosen? **When God binds our wounds, we are set free**. We are no longer bound to them! Oh friend, I just see the chains being loosened, the hearts being set free! Let God heal your heart. Let Him permeate you and drench you with His healing touch, His love! His love is unconditional, immutable, all powerful, enduring, unending, endearing, sacrificial, unfailing, unchanging, forgiving and forever! But don't take my word for it. Find out for yourself. Dive in to His Word. Spend time talking to Him as you would a treasured friend. Spend time with Him just abiding, with no other purpose but to be in His presence. Just as the woman who was healed simply by seeking Him out to touch His garment, so you too will be healed simply by seeking His presence.

The thing to remember is that healing the wounds takes time. There are many layers to peel back. I promise you if you take these three steps of opening your heart to Jesus, stepping out in faith to forgive those who have hurt you, and allowing God to bathe you in His unfathomable love, it will put you on the path of learning to abandon your heart to God which leads to a life of complete freedom and fulfillment.

~ Chapter 7~

Abandoning Your Heart

If you return to the LORD with all your heart...He will deliver you ~ I Samuel 7:3 ~

One thing that you will come to discover is that learning to abandon your heart to God is a process. It is a lifelong journey. It is not a one-time event or a revelation that changes your life all at once. It is something that we must choose to walk out daily. I want to stress this, my friend, WE MUST CHOOSE, and when we fail, as most of us will, we just get back up and try again. God is a God of second chances. I am living proof of that!

On this journey of abandoning our hearts to God, we must choose to obey His instructions. Again, His commands are not prohibitive. They are designed to protect our hearts. If we obey His commands we severely limit the chance of future wounds that will need to go through the healing process. We must understand that God, as our Father, wants to nurture us, teach us, and discipline us and that it is all for our own good. I always hated it when I was a kid and my mother would tell me right before she would spank me "this is for your own good." While as a child I didn't understand it, I have come to realize that there is some truth in those words. Just as parents discipline their children or have rules for their children, God has the same for us. As parents, we don't enforce the rules or discipline our children because we simply want to or to stop our children from having fun. No, we do it because we love them so much. We want what is best for them. God does the same for us, only as hard as it is to imagine, God's love is far, far greater than any love that we could have for our children. Many of us, when we hear the word discipline, shut down. Our view of discipline is not a positive one, but I don't think discipline, in the true sense of the word, is meant to have the connotation that many of us associate with it. The root word of discipline is disciple. *Disciple* means to teach or to train. Sure, discipline involves negative consequences and correction sometimes, but the majority of discipline involves training and that is where God's instructions come in. He is training us to become more like Him. 2 Timothy 3:16 says *"All Scripture is God-breathed and is useful for teaching, rebuking, correcting and training in righteousness."* Hebrews 12:11 says *"No discipline seems pleasant at the time, but painful. Later on, however, it produces a harvest of righteousness and peace for those who have been trained by it."* There it is my friend! Do you see it? There is peace for those who have been trained by discipline. So as we learn to obey God's instructions, and allow God to

DISCIPLinE us, we become more righteous and with righteousness comes peace!

We must also learn on this journey what is spoken in Psalm 51:

Have mercy on me, O God,
according to your unfailing love;
according to your great compassion
blot out my transgressions.
Wash away all my iniquity
and cleanse me from my sin.

For I know my transgressions,
and my sin is always before me.
Against you, you only, have I sinned
and done what is evil in your sight;
so you are right on your verdict
and justified when you judge.
Surely I was sinful at birth,
sinful from the time my mother conceived me.
Yet you desired faithfulness even in the womb;
you taught me wisdom in that secret place.

Cleanse me with hyssop, and I will be clean;
wash me, and I will be whiter than snow.
Let me hear joy and gladness;
let the bones you have crushed rejoice.
Hide your face from my sins
and blot out all my iniquity.

Create in me a pure heart, O God,
and renew a steadfast spirit within me.
Do not cast me from your presence
or take your Holy Spirit from me.
Restore to me the joy of your salvation
and grant me a willing spirit, to sustain me.

Then I will teach transgressors your ways,
and sinners will turn back to you.

Save me from blood guilt, O God,
the God who saves me,
and my tongue will sing of your righteousness.
O Lord, open my lips,
and my mouth will declare your praise.
You do not delight in sacrifice, or I would bring it;
you do not take pleasure in burnt offerings.
My sacrifice, O God, is a broken spirit;
a broken and contrite heart,
O God, you will not despise...

This is David, after defiling Bathsheba and then killing her husband, getting on his knees before God, recognizing that he is a sinner, asking God to cleanse his heart, make it pure and fill him with His Holy Spirit. We must choose, no matter what, to come before God every single day seeking forgiveness for our sins and asking for God to fill us with His Spirit. One thing that I have learned is that going through each day without being filled with the Spirit of God makes for a difficult day. My emotions are in control instead of the Spirit of God. My wounds seem to resurface. My perception gets all out of sorts. In order to learn to abandon our hearts to God, we must spend time in His presence, talking with Him and building a strong relationship with Him. If we are interested in really getting to know someone we spend a lot of time with them, talking, listening and just hanging out. It's the same with our LORD. If you want to know Him just hang out with Him and if you need answers, just ask. God speaks to us through His Word, through other believers and through that still small voice. It is hard to recognize at first but the more time you spend with Him, the easier it gets. Think about it this way: if I were to call you on the phone right now, you would probably respond with "Who is this?" You don't know my voice because you haven't spent any time communicating with me. But after a few weeks of speaking every day, you will probably no longer have to ask. You would immediately recognize my voice because you have been speaking with me regularly. In the same way, at first you may not recognize God's voice, but keep spending time with Him, keep the conversation going and eventually you won't have to ask "God, is that you?" You will begin to recognize His voice. Spending time with God cleansing our hearts, readdressing our wounds, allowing Him to fill you with His Spirit, is crucial in your journey of abandonment.

You will also see in this Scripture that David's sacrifice to God is a broken spirit; a broken and contrite heart. Contrite simply means that our hearts are repentant. Broken is when we come before God without pride, putting self aside and saying "Here I am God. I am yours completely, willing to do whatever you ask." When we come before God with a broken and contrite heart, He looks upon us with favor and through us can accomplish great things (Isaiah 66:2). Noah, who was a drunk, found favor, and his family was saved from the destruction of the flood. Abraham, who longed for children and decided to get them his way instead of waiting on God, found favor and he became the father of many nations. Joseph, who was sold by his brothers into slavery because of his pride and spent years in prison falsely accused, found favor and he became second in line to the Pharaoh in Egypt. David found favor and he became king. You see, all of these people had a past, yet through God's redemption, they found favor! I wonder what God will do through you as He looks upon you with favor?

Also necessary on this journey of abandoning our hearts completely to God is that we must learn to love the way that He loves. Again, this is something that we must choose daily. As we have discovered in previous chapters, love is a choice, not a feeling. There are going to be plenty of times that we are not going to feel like loving but God instructs us to love Him with all of our heart, soul, mind and strength and to love our neighbor as we love ourselves. In fact He says that out of all the commandments that He gives, love is the greatest! So how do we do it? How do we love others the way that He wants? Well, I will tell you that it is impossible without the first two. We can't love the way that He does unless we understand obedience and unless we are getting to know Him and learning what His love is like. Learning how deeply He loves us and how much He wants us to love ourselves. It is impossible to give away what we do not have ourselves, so if we are not receiving the love of God and allowing it to fill us, then we cannot pour it out onto others.

The journey is not always easy, friends, but it is worth every ounce of energy that you have to put toward it and frankly it's easier than any other path you could choose without God. It is not always enjoyable either. Let's face it: we can really screw things up. We are human, after all, and consequences aren't always fun. When we do mess up, however, we have to learn to lean into Him and allow Him to pick us up again. Allow Him to teach us through our pain. It will ensure a joy-filled, bright future for you, your family and everyone else that is blessed to call you friend, and will cause you to love others the way God intended by loving them where they are without expecting anything in return because God has given you all you need. No matter the circumstances there will be trust, hope and joy because God first loved us right where we were and still loves us right where we are now! The good news is that He loves us enough not to leave us here and walks with us every step of the way on this journey called LIFE and you, my friend, can Live In Freedom Everyday!

~Chapter 8~

The Generous Heart

In everything I did, I showed you that by this kind of hard work we must help the weak, remembering the words the Lord Jesus Himself said: "It is more blessed to give than to receive." ~ Acts 20:35 ~

More blessed to give than receive…countercultural to say the least, yet that is what God calls us to do. If you have been on this journey with us, abandoning your heart to the Father, then you have, no doubt, received so much yourself. You see, God wants us to take our now awakened, unveiled, circumcised and healed hearts to show Him and His love to a hurting world out there! Just as we once were, there are women out there desperately searching for something more; wanting more than anything to be called worthy. Again, this path will be different for all of us but we can search God and His heart for His plan for us.

Generous with our time

One of the ways that we can have a generous heart is with our time. Unfortunately we have busy lives because we live in a culture that promotes busyness and this leaves many of us with no margin for giving back. I believe that busyness is Satan's way of keeping us from many things, including our relationship with God and others as well as giving back in our communities. God commands us in 1 Timothy to do good, be rich in good deeds, and to be generous and willing to share.

I remember the day I met my friend Julie. I was her new cubby mate at work and I am sure she recognized immediately what an absolute mess I was. It was never an "official" mentoring relationship but she took me by the hand, guided me through big decisions and was always there for me when I had questions. She would stop anything if I said I needed her and there is not a doubt in my mind that she would do it again and again. I see her still doing it today with women who need it. She gives so much of her time to others, mentoring them, teaching them how to live a life worthy of being called a follower of Jesus. She lives Romans 12:9-13. Her love is always sincere. She hates what is evil, even if it is in me and she has to call me out on it. She loves what is good and loves to show others how to do good by the power that is at work within them. She is completely devoted to me in love, even when it hurts, and she honors me above herself. She often puts her own needs aside for me. She never lacks in zeal and spiritual fervor and spends her life serving the LORD. She remains joyful in hope, patient in affliction and faithful in prayer and constantly reminds me to do the same. She has been a faithful example of walking through trials and deep, deep pain, trusting the LORD with all of her heart, soul, mind and strength and has willingly taught me the same as she generously gave of her time to me through mentoring.

This has been one of the most crucial elements in my walk with the LORD; someone to walk with me through it all. If you don't have a mentor, I highly recommend you seeking one out. Then, it is said, you only have to be one step ahead to help someone else. See where you can step in and help another who is struggling. Our service to others puts us in a place of realizing that we are not alone but more than that, it helps someone else know they are not alone. Before we know it, if we are allowing God to work, our pain is less and our purpose is clear. We begin sharing God to a world that needs Him.

Generous with our talents

Another way that we can have generous hearts is through our talents. God has wired all of us so differently. The problem is when you have spent your life feeling unworthy and useless like I had, it becomes difficult to see what your talents are. It took well over 10 years after this process for me begin believing that I actually had something to contribute to the Kingdom work that was being done here on earth. I had been serving in ministry for 7 years before I truly believed I was called. To me, it was a job that I was extremely grateful for, but a calling…well I wasn't convinced of that. It wasn't until I was healed and my heart wasn't being deceived any longer that I was able to accept the truth about who I am. You see, God's word says that you are His child and are chosen by Him (John 1:12). You are a branch of the True Vine and are to be a conduit of His love (John 15). It says that you have been justified and redeemed (Romans 3:24) and you are no longer slave to sin (Romans 6:6). Your body is a temple for the Holy Spirit (I Corinthians 6:19) and that you are one in Spirit with Him (I Corinthians 6:17). It reminds you that you are chosen, holy and blameless; redeemed and forgiven (Ephesians 1). Sweet sister, you are God's workmanship, created to produce good works (Ephesians 2:10) and to boldly and confidently access God through faith in Christ Jesus (Ephesians 3:12). All of these truths prove that you are chosen by Him to influence and partake in kingdom work and with the knowledge and assurance of knowing who you are in Christ we can confidently find our place in that work.

For me, God led me to start and organization for single mothers. Romans 8:28 says that "in all things, God works for the good of those who love Him, who have been called according to His purpose". And that is exactly what he did for me. He used my tumultuous past so that not a shred of it will have been lived in vain, and started an organization to help moms who are where I have been. He has given me a passion for these sweet moms and a desire to show them how God can change their lives; a longing to show them that they don't have to be defined by their circumstances or stay where they are; that there is hope for their future and a better life for their families. As I prayed about what to call the organization that God had called me start, He gave me the name MAIA, which means "great mother" in Greek. He wants these moms to know that they have the potential to be a great mom because no one has ever told them that. He wants these moms to find hope in Him so they can be restored and redeemed and pass on that legacy to their children. This is the small piece of Kingdom work for me and He has it for you too. You too are called according to His purposes.

As we move forward into our calling and belief that we are called we have to remember that it is God who works in and through us. Too many times, as many wounded women do, I have defaulted to relying on my own strength to sustain this task that the LORD has given me only to find myself burned out, stretched thin and too exhausted to continue. Too many times I have had to repent for not relying on God to sustain me DAILY! Girls, our default is going to be to do it ourselves. After all, we have been let down too many times by others. But I promise, we won't be let down by God.

Your work is not going to be the same as mine. After all, He created you to be you. But in this you can be rest assured...He does have a calling for you. He has work for you to do. If people along the years hadn't shared God's love and life change, I wouldn't be writing this book and you certainly wouldn't be reading it because I wouldn't know God and you can't pass on what you don't have.

I encourage you to pray about your calling. What does God want you to do? It took ten years after my divorce to even consider what God might have planned for me. I had to become whole. I needed healing first. It took the Apostle Paul 14 years after his encounter with Jesus on the road to Damascus to begin his ministry. Let the LORD do His great work within you and then, as you move forward, let Him reveal His plan for you. Don't do something just because it's there to do. That just might be for someone else. Do what only you can do. God has you here for a purpose. It may be simply parenting the children that He has already entrusted you with. This is, after all, the most magnificent and crucial job on the planet. It may be mentoring, as it is with my friend Julie, or lending a helping hand to someone in need. But whatever it is, if done for the Glory of God, you will not be disappointed. He has a plan for you and you alone! Believe that, trust in His plan and provision for that plan. He is able!

~ Chapter 9 ~

The Praying Heart

Then you will call on me and come and pray to me, and I will listen to you.
~ Jeremiah 29:12 ~

One of the most important and valuable things that you can do on this journey is PRAY! It is how we communicate with our Creator. This has been one of my biggest struggles. I would either not know what to say or I would often wonder if I was praying God's will or my own. The best solution for both of these problems, I have discovered, is praying Scripture. Now as I am reading God's word during my quiet time, I am always thinking about how this can apply to me or my family. Here is how it looks at times for me. These are real life prayers from my own prayer journal:

My Reading:

Psalm 150:1-2 ~ Praise God in His sanctuary, praise Him in His mighty heavens. Praise Him for His acts of power, praise Him for His surpassing greatness.

My Prayer:

I will praise You forever God. Praise You for what You have done for my family, for the way You have transformed me and my life. Help me to remember all the things You have done for us. I will praise You in the trials, believing that Your power is at work and Your greatness will surpass all things.

My Reading:

Philippians 1 and 2 ~ from the NIV

My Prayer:

LORD, thank You for growth. As painful as it is I know it is necessary. Thank You for using my life to bring You glory. I pray that my love may abound more and more in knowledge and depth of insight so that I am able to discern what is best and that I may be pure and blameless. I pray that I do nothing out of selfish ambition or vain conceit. That I would remain humble and consider everyone else better than myself; that I would look to the interests of others without fear of rejection and without expectations. That I would learn from You the agape love that You show to us every day. Give me strength in that. One of the hardest things that I have tried and have yet to accomplish is to lay myself aside for the benefit of others. My selfishness always gets in the way. I focus on my hurt, my pain, my desire and my fears rather than laying those aside and focusing on You. Guide me Jesus. I cannot do this without You!

There have been other times where I have simply prayed the desires of my heart only to see the provision of our Father just a short time later:

8/18/04 – this prayer came on my sweet middle child's third birthday while I was at the end of my rope with him.

Lord save me! I cannot do this alone. I am overwhelmed, frustrated, angry and sad. I just don't know how much longer I can do this. Every day I have these feelings and every day I repent for them. How much longer must I continue in this cycle? The overwhelming task of being a single parent is wearing me down. I am so grateful for these beautiful souls You have entrusted to me, yet at the same time I am angry for having to do this alone. I am angry at myself for making so many poor decisions. I am angry that they don't have the father that they deserve. I am so guilty of giving You my burdens, then taking them right back from You. Thank You for Your grace. I commit my children to You AGAIN. They are Your children first. I need You Father. I cannot endure this without You.

This was written in my journal while locked in my room after overreacting in anger toward my middle son. He was being quite difficult, as he often was during these years, and I remember putting my hands around his neck. My anger had gotten the best of me. Fortunately I had enough sense to move my hands to his head where I couldn't hurt him. This was a very dark time for me. I was desperate to be a good mom but too angry and overwhelmed to know how. So after nearly choking him, I locked myself in my room so that I could compose myself and figure out how to do it better…and pray, even though praying was the last thing I felt like doing at the moment. Shortly after writing this, I met Gary and Anne Marie Ezzo, parenting experts and authors of many parenting books, who have walked with me every step of the way since. They taught me how to be a successful single parent. They had just moved to South Carolina from California, and while they had other reasons for moving here, I am convinced this was God's provision just for me.

12/16/08 – after years of struggling with the boys in school I was desperate and at my wits end.

Lord, thank You for turning my focus back to my children. I have been preoccupied. Forgive me. Thank You for the many amazing blessings that You have given us; our home, my job and our family. God I feel like I have so much and am in need of nothing yet I sit here requesting from You. This school thing is really affecting me LORD. It doesn't seem to be affecting the boys and I know their minds don't understand what mine does and their hearts don't feel what I feel. LORD, I do not ever want to be blinded to the shortcomings and misbehavior of my children. Please protect me from that. Keep the veil removed from my eyes and allow me to see their sin. I believe that these situations at the school have been blown out of proportion. Why has school been so hard for us LORD? Are You trying to show me something or is the enemy trying to invade? I need Your guidance Father. Show me what to do next. If it is Your will for us to stay then I will trust You with that, regardless of how it looks to me on the surface. If we are to move to another school, possibly a Christian school, then I trust You to provide the way; A clear path to our destination.

As you can see, I inserted a little of my own will in there (possibly a Christian School) but I also believe that God wants to give us the desires of our hearts as long as they don't conflict with His will. Literally just a few months later, a couple at our church came up to me after service and asked to speak with me. They said they had been praying for my family and felt as if the LORD was asking them to send my children to private school or pay me to homeschool them because as a single parent they knew that I couldn't go without an income. I couldn't believe it. Even though my prayers were real and I believed that God was in control, I was shocked that this is how He would do it. He actually spoke to someone else who had no idea that I was praying those prayers and provided through them. They are still attending private Christian school today and are flourishing like I have never seen them flourish.

I tell you these stories so you can see that **God answers prayers**! He is a God of provision! He is a faithful God! He is a God who knows better than I what is best for me! This doesn't mean that God's answers to prayers are always yes. While our sweet Father loves to provide for us and He loves to show off His faithfulness, there are times that no is the better answer. My children struggle with this one. I think many children, and even adults, do. They believe that God doesn't answer prayer when really God is just saying no.

My son Benjamin asked me the other day why he didn't win his basketball game. He had prayed really hard that they would win. I would even see him at the free throw line with his hands folded, praying just before his teammate would shoot the ball. I was over in the stands desperately wanting God to honor my precious boy for his willingness to pray so openly. I was praying "Oh God, show him your faithfulness. Build his faith by answering his prayers." Yet they never won a game that season.

One of the greatest answers to prayer that I have received is the treasured man I now call husband. After almost ten years of being a single parent, years after I began writing this book, He has given me someone to walk alongside in life. Someone who puts God first in everything he does, who is not afraid to lead my family, who helps me be a better person, a better parent and who takes on all of the parenting responsibilities for three children who aren't biologically his. Strangers would never know that they don't belong to him. It is so much more than I could have ever imagined and honestly, I would have settled for much less because I still struggle with my value and worth (yes, I am still on the journey too), but I believe because of my commitment to God, He wouldn't allow it. I tell you this to help you understand why God says no sometimes. My children have fallen madly in love with my new husband. The two younger ones asked just minutes after we said "I do" if they could call him daddy. So when my son Benjamin asked me about not winning the game I asked him:

"Ben, how much do you love Rob (the hubby)?"

"A lot" he said.

"Well, aren't you glad that God gave him to us?"

"Yes, very much, I couldn't imagine life without him now Mom."

"Well, Benjamin, several years ago I was dating a man that you really didn't know about. I really, really liked him, and I was begging God to let me marry him. If God had said yes, then Rob wouldn't be here with us today. Wouldn't that be sad"?

…and Benjamin began to understand that when God says no, it is not because He doesn't answer prayers, it is because He has something much better planned.

So, my friend, will you commit yourself to prayer? God is so faithful and true and just. He may say no sometimes but just trust Him! He knows what is best for you, His precious daughter whom He loves deeply.

Here is a quick, simple acronym that someone taught me. It helps me remember how to pray:

A – *Adoration*. Tell God how good He is, how much you adore and treasure Him. How much you trust Him and believe in Him.

C – *Confession*. Confess your sins. Let Him cleanse you and make your heart clean.

T – *Thanksgiving*. Thank Him for all the things He has done. For answered prayer, even when the answer has been NO. For your children, friends, family and more.

S – *Supplication*. This is where we ask for our needs to be met. For the desires of our hearts to be delivered.

Blessings to you sweet sister. May your journey be joyous, fulfilling and eye-opening as you seek our Father, through His Son Jesus, who will give you whatever you need to let go of your past and step into a life that is healed and restored as you abandon your heart to His plan for your life! Let's commit to living with a HEART ABANDONED to the Spirit of God because where the Spirit of God is there is FREEDOM! Bless you!

~ Chapter 10 ~

Prayers for the Heart

So is My word...it will not return to me empty, but will accomplish what I desire.

~ Isaiah 55:11 ~

As I have said, I am a firm, firm believer in praying scripture. Prayer is not simply a matter of asking God for what we want and expecting Him to give it to us. He is not Santa Clause. HE IS GOD! I have learned the hard way that what I want is not always God's best for me so when I pray, I want to be certain that I am praying God's will and not my own and the best way to do that is to pray scripture...the living, breathing, life-altering Word of God.

People have often asked me "how do I know if I am praying God's will?" I always, without fail, tell them to find Scripture to pray over the situation. This chapter is designed to do just that: give you situations that you may find yourself in and show you how to pray Scripture over them. This is the part of the book that you will want to regularly refer back to as you learn to search Scripture yourself. My goal is to give you some of the Scriptures related to each situation and one example of how I would pray this Scripture and help you learn how to do that yourself; then give you other Scriptures that will guide you in your own prayers. I encourage you to search the Word of God yourself. His Word does not return void and if you search, you WILL find!

Feeling Unloved or Lonely

Psalm 143:8 – Let the morning bring me word of your unfailing love, for I have put my trust in you.

Lord- your word says that you have an unfailing love for me but I don't feel love. I am lonely and frustrated but I choose to put my trust in you. Show me your love for me today. Let me see it so clearly that I can't deny that it is from you. In Jesus Name.

Ephesians 1:4-5 – For He chose us in Him before the creation of the world to be holy and blameless in His sight. In love He predestined us for adoption to sonship through Jesus Christ, in accordance with His pleasure and will.

Romans 8:37 – No, in all these things we are more than conquerors through Him who loved us. For I am convinced that neither death nor life, neither angels nor demons, neither the present nor the future, nor any powers, neither height nor depth, nor anything else in all creation, will be able to separate us from the love of God that is in Christ Jesus our LORD.

Proverbs 4:23 – Above all else, guard your heart, for everything you do flows from it.

Wanting to know God's Will

Psalm 143:10 – Teach me to do your will, for you are my God; may your good Spirit lead me on level ground.

God, your word says that your Spirit will lead me on level ground. Please help me to know your will. Teach me to do your will. You are my God and I trust in you. I need to know what you want in this situation and I am trusting in your guidance. In Jesus Name.

Colossians 2:2-3 – My goal is that they may be encouraged in heart and united in love, so that they may have the full riches of complete understanding, in order that they may know the mystery of God, namely, Christ, in whom are hidden all treasures of wisdom and knowledge.

Psalm 37:7 – Be still before the LORD and wait patiently for Him

Proverbs 3:1 – My son, do not forget my teaching, but keep my commands in your heart.

Romans 12:2 – do not conform to the pattern of this world, but be transformed by the renewing of your mind. Then you will be able to test and approve what God's will is – His good, pleasing and perfect will.

Psalms 48:14 – For this God is our God for ever and ever; He will be our guide even to the end.

When I am afraid

2 Timothy 1:7 – For the Spirit God gave us does not make us timid, but gives us power, love and self-discipline.

LORD, you say that it is your Spirit that makes me not afraid. I am really scared right now and I need you. Give me your power because of your love and give me strength to make it through. In Jesus Name.

Philippians 4:6-7 – Do not be anxious about anything, but in every situation, by prayer and petition, with thanksgiving, present your requests to God. And the peace of God, which transcends all understanding, will guard your hearts and your minds in Christ Jesus.

Psalm 23:4 – Even though I walk through the darkest valley, I will fear no evil, for you are with me; your rod and your staff they comfort me.

Isaiah 41:13 – For I am the LORD your God who takes hold of your right hand and says to you, do not fear; I will help you.

When I have a need

Romans 12:12 – Be joyful in hope, patient in affliction, faithful in prayer.

God, I have a great need. I know that you are fully aware of my needs before I even know and therefore my hope is in you. I choose joy while I am waiting for your provision and wait patiently for your answer. In Jesus Name.

Philippians 4:11 – I am not saying this because I am in need, for I have learned to be content whatever the circumstances.

Psalms 37:4-6 – Take delight in the LORD, and He will give you the desires of your heart. Commit your way to the LORD; trust in Him and He will do this: He will make your righteous reward shine like the dawn…

Psalms 27:8 – My heart says of you, "seek His face!" Your face LORD, I will seek.

When I am struggling with sin

Matthew 26:41 – Watch and pray so that you will not fall into temptation. The spirit is willing, but the flesh is weak

LORD, I desperately want to obey you in this matter but every time I find myself in this situation, I fail. Forgive me for my sin Father. My flesh is weak even though I want nothing more than to obey you. Give me the tools I need to know how to keep watch and LORD honor my prayers. In Jesus Name.

Psalm 37:23-24 – The LORD makes firm the steps of the one who delights in Him; thought he may stumble, he will not fall, for the LORD upholds him with His hand.

Proverbs 3:11-12 – My son (daughter) do not despise the LORD's discipline, and do not resent His rebuke, because the LORD disciplines those He loves...

Romans 8:2 – Because through Christ Jesus the law of the Spirit who gives life has set you free from the law of sin and death.

Proverbs 15:31 – Whoever heeds life-giving correction will be at home among the wise.

When I am sad or depressed

Colossians 2:6-7 – So then, just as you received Christ Jesus as LORD, continue to live your lives in Him, rooted and built up in Him, strengthened in the faith as you were taught, and overflowing with thankfulness.

LORD, you know my heart. It is so heavy with sadness right now. Because I am rooted in you, I choose thankfulness for my situation I know thankfulness and sadness can't live together so remove the sadness from my heart, In Jesus Name.

Psalms 119:28 – I weep with sorrow; encourage me by your word.

Psalms 30:5 - …weeping may stay for the night, but rejoicing comes in the morning.

Isaiah 61:7 – Instead of shame you will receive a double portion, and instead of disgrace you will rejoice in your inheritance. And so you will inherit a double portion in your land, and everlasting joy will be yours.

2 Corinthians 8:2 – In the midst of a very severe trial, their overflowing joy and their extreme poverty welled up in rich generosity.

1 John 4:4 – You, dear children, are from God and have overcome them, because the one who is in you is greater than the one who is in the world.

When struggling with pride

John 3:30 – He must become greater; I must become less

LORD, I am really struggling here. I am embarrassed and ashamed that I am going through life this way. This is not how I thought it would be. God I know this is not about me, but about you. Help me to look to you in every situation, no matter how I feel. Show me how to glorify you and make you greater and teach me not to concern myself with what others may think. In Jesus Name.

1 Corinthians 3:18-19 – Do not deceive yourselves. If any of you think you are wise by the standards of this age, you should become "fools" so that you may become wise. For the wisdom of this world is foolishness in God's sight.

Proverbs 11:2 - When pride comes, then comes disgrace, but with humility comes wisdom.

When I have been hurt

Romans 12:14 – Bless those who persecute you; bless and do not curse.

Mark 11:25 – And when you stand praying, if you hold anything against anyone, forgive them, so that your Father in heaven may forgive you your sins.

LORD, I am really struggling to forgive _____. She has hurt me deeply and I don't know how to forgive. Your Word says that I need to forgive before I come to you so even though I don't feel like forgiving, I confess right now that I choose to forgive and trust you with the rest. I recognize that forgiveness is for me and not the one who wronged me so help me Father to walk in forgiveness when my flesh is weak. In Jesus Name!

Ephesians 2:26-27 – In your anger do not sin. Do not let the sun go down while you are still angry, and do not give the devil a foothold.

Friends, as we continue on this path, I encourage you to remember that abandoning your heart fully is a process. Keep seeking Him, keep praying, keep reading His Word and you will become rooted in His love and with that NOTHING IS IMPOSSIBLE. Godspeed sisters!

Discover More at...

http://allisonherrin.com

http://maiamoms.org

www.ingramcontent.com/pod-product-compliance
Lightning Source LLC
Chambersburg PA
CBHW032007040426

42448CB00006B/521